THICK VILLAINS

The Criminals so Stupid
They Catch Themselves

THICK VILLAINS

The Criminals so Stupid
They Catch Themselves

Simon Vigar

Foreword by Jamie Theakston

PORTICO

First published in the United Kingdom in 2007 by
Portico Books
10 Southcombe Street
London
W14 0RA

An imprint of Anova Books Company Ltd

Illustrations by Oxford Designers & Illustrators

ISBN 9781906032210

A CIP catalogue record for this book is available from the British
Library.

10 9 8 7 6 5 4 3 2 1

Printed and bound by MPG Books Ltd, Bodmin, Cornwall

This book can be ordered direct from the publisher.
Contact the marketing department, but try your bookshop first.

www.anovabooks.com

For Elizabeth & Ella

CONTENTS

ACKNOWLEDGEMENTS

Thanks very much to Jamie Theakston, Harriet Scott and the whole team at Heart Breakfast for putting up with my nonsense and giving me the oxygen of publicity; to Mark Browning, Francis Currie, Phil Riley and Richard Huntingford, the non-suited 'suits' at Heart 106.2 for indulging me; to Barnaby Dawe at Heart for believing in the book and making everything happen; to Jonathan Lloyd for his invaluable advice on the strange world of publishing; to Tom Bromley and Malcolm Croft at Portico and Polly Powell at Anova for making it less strange and being incredibly supportive; to Jonathan Richards and Jono Coleman for their friendship, and to my girls, Elizabeth and Ella, for their understanding and their love.

But most of all thank-you to the thick villains of the world.

You lot make my job easy.

FOREWORD

By Jamie Theakston

I've been trying to get this feature banned from the Heart Breakfast show for years now, but Simon keeps coming back with the same ropey old material. He says it's funny, the producer says it's cheap, so it gets on. When I signed up for a flagship show in one of the world's toughest radio markets, absolutely no-one had the guts to tell me I'd be lugging around the dead weight of Simon and his endless thick villains. Frankly, it's a minor miracle we're London's number one rated breakfast show and anyone buying this book needs to take a good look at how they organise their finances. Anyway, to the 'contractual obligation' part of this foreword ...

True stories of stupid criminals make everyone smile; it makes you feel a bit better about the world. In this book you'll hear of the bank robber armed only with a banana, the raider who was taken out by a gang of pensioners and the man who selected a tractor as his getaway vehicle of choice.

And who could forget (it says here) the robber who was run over by his own getaway car, the mugger chased for miles by a marathon runner and the several burglars who forgot that air vents only work as escape routes in the movies.

A personal favourite is the mugger who vaulted a wall during his getaway... and landed in a tiger enclosure. Out of the frying pan ...

There, don't you feel better about being a law-abiding citizen? In all seriousness, it's been a great pleasure to have Simon finding these stories for us. Oh, and one other thing ... the thick villain who stole the manuscript of this book and got it published is still at large ...

July 2007

Introduction

By Simon Vigar

I think the Chinese philosopher Juang-zu spoke for us all when he said, 'I don't 'alf love those true stories about thick villains, guv, they crease me up somethin' rotten. Milk with two sugars, please.' There is something in those elegant and, admittedly, invented words.

Of all the 'and finally' stories I do, I've always had a soft spot for my thick villains. They just keep on coming, proving that most of them are forced into a life of crime through sheer stupidity. Despite what Hollywood tells you, there are very few dashing, criminal masterminds out there and, by definition, we don't know about or can't convict the exceptional few.

If you've ever been tempted to pack in the whole law-abiding, tax-paying game, read on. Most crime is fuelled by drink and drugs but, I have to say, law breakers would increase their chances if they just cut down a bit during their criminal operations. The number of them who just pass out while 'on the job' is almost embarrassing. Equally, drink and drugs impair judgement. For example, trying to sell drugs to a uniformed police officer is literally asking for trouble and, burglars, if its snowing, don't just walk straight back home.

Modern technology is also playing it's role as people are able to watch CCTV remotely and track mobile-phone records. We also have a special mention for the 'smarter sex'. The female section may be as small as Paris Hilton's cell but its no less interesting for that. We finally salute a few smart villains who've totally outclassed the law-enforcement authorities.

I suppose my favourite thick villains are the ones who think they're being really clever. Like the (male) idiot who thought a good alibi would be a stolen letter for an appointment with a gynaecologist. Or the bank robbers who believed they had prepared for every eventuality until they jumped into the getaway car to find the fuel tank empty.

You couldn't make it up and, happily, you don't have to. As the 17th-century French satirist Jean de La Bruyère wisely said, 'If poverty is the mother of crime, stupidity is its father.'

No, he really did.

THICK VILLAINS

AMERICAN IDIOT

Thick villainy is truly international but, it must be said, my happiest hunting ground for stories is the good old U S of A. Of course, with 275 million citizens the story count is bound to be higher; but why not even more stories from China, India or Russia? It's partly a language thing but also because there are many more media outlets in the USA.

A few stories sometimes do reach me from those huge countries I've mentioned but there is always a bigger question mark over their veracity. Sometimes the stories are simply too good to be true or maybe they lose something in translation.

Anyway, what I'm trying to get at here is there are lots of thick villains in the USA.

Have a good laugh, y'all.

A CRASH COURSE IN IDIOCY: PART ONE

Catching drug dealers can take years of police time: man-hour after man-hour of surveillance, interviews and stakeouts before an arrest can even be made. At the other end of the scale though there are thick villains who take to helping the police with their enquiries to a new and bizarre level.

When one drug dealer in South Carolina got so high on his own stash, crashing his car, he thought, would be the least of his worries. Not true, however, as the car he crashed into was a [*drum roll please*] ... a police car! Bad? Well, things were not over yet ...

Officers in South Carolina say it was their easiest ever drugs bust. Why? The car was laden with a stash of marijuana worth $75,000 ... and, of course, one prize dope.

The driver has been charged.

A CRASH COURSE IN IDIOCY: PART TWO

There comes a point in life when you just have to admit your mistakes.

Many of us have been in a similar situation to the one that a 35-year-old man in California recently found himself in – pranging a partner's car and being desperate for them not to find out. Few of us, though, have taken his next step – attempting to fake his own kidnapping to get out of the situation.

The man told Californian police that he'd been held at gun-point by two men and had been forced to crash the car into a wall in order to escape. Strangely enough, there was no sign of the two gunmen ... and anyone who believed the story. The man, incredibly, faces charges for faking his own kidnapping.

As for what his wife planned for him when he got home is another thing entirely ...

YOU'RE UNDER ARREST! NO, *YOU'RE* UNDER ARREST!

It's one thing to play 'cops and robbers' when you're growing up. But trying it on in adult life can have somewhat more severe consequences.

Marvin Williams thought it would be funny to put a blue-and-red flashing light on the dashboard of his friend's car and pretend to pull over another motorist. So far, so hilarious. But the joke backfired when Williams picked a car with two undercover Tampa cops inside. Doh!

It got worse. Marvin ran from the vehicle, leaving behind two female friends ... and seven grams of cocaine.

Marvin is helping the real police with their enquiries.

He may be some time.

OH, SHOOT

What's worse than a gun that doesn't work? A gun that doesn't work *sometimes* ...

When his 38-calibre revolver failed to fire at his intended victim during a hold-up in Long Beach, California, wannabe robber James Elliot did something that can only inspire wonder. He peered down the barrel and tried the trigger again. This time, tragically, it worked.

SHORT CHANGED

This is the story of a store that was held up, and came away with a profit.

A man walked into a Louisiana Circle-K, put a $20 bill on the counter, and asked for change. When the clerk opened the cash drawer, the man pulled a gun and asked for all the cash in the register, which the clerk promptly provided. The man took the cash from the clerk and fled, leaving the $20 bill on the counter. The total amount of cash he got from the drawer: $15.

I'm at a loss too.

FUNFACT:

America puts many more of its citizens in prison than any other nation.

A GOOD IDEA GONE TO POO

Stealing petrol from someone else's tank is not the most glamorous crime ever invented. And that's before you put your hose in the wrong hole by mistake.

When a man attempted to siphon petrol from a motor home parked on a Seattle street, he got much more than he bargained for. Police arrived at the scene to find a very sick man curled up next to a motor home near spilled sewage.

A police spokesman reported that the man admitted to trying to steal petrol and plugged his siphon hose into the motor home's sewage tank by mistake. The owner of the vehicle declined to press charges, saying that it was the best laugh he'd ever had.

At least someone was having a gas.

YOU WANT P45s WITH THAT?

Over to Boise, Idaho for the slowest joyride in the world ...

Two staff at the local ice rink were sacked for nicking the ice re-surfacing machines and going to a Burger King drive-thru.

It wasn't difficult to catch up with these particular thickos though: the machines have a top speed of 5mph and the boys had to travel about a mile and a half. Not so much 'on the run' as 'on the walk'.

Local parks director Jim Hall told the *Guardian*: 'It was one of the five stupidest things I've ever seen.'

Annoyingly, he doesn't tell what the other four were.

PIPE DOWN!

Not so much a thick villain here as one with quite a bit of front ...

When Dana Roberts held up a car-parts shop in Rochester, he thought he'd made a clean getaway with the cash. But he hadn't reckoned on two employees chasing him and then proceeding to beat him with a metal pipe to get the money back. Now Roberts is suing the two employees for assault and causing him emotional distress, claiming their actions were 'unnecessary'.

I don't recall Moriarity ever making the same claims against Sherlock Holmes.

GETAWAY KARMA

A group of thieves in Florida clearly don't believe in Karma because they've stolen a 600lb gold statue of Buddha from a restaurant.

One of the central precepts of Buddhism is `Do not take what is not yours to take'. Buddhists also believe a person's actions in this life determine the quality of their existence in the next.

One can only hope for these thieves' sake that Richard Dawkins is right.

Otherwise, we reckon they might be finding themselves reincarnated underneath a 600lb gold statue of Buddha!

AND NOW FOR SOMETHING COMPLETELY STUPID ...

If you think you know someone who's stubborn, how about this ...?

68-year-old H Beatty Chadwick from Philadelphia has spent 11 years in jail because he refuses to tell his ex-wife what happened to his fortune.

The *Philadelphia Times* reported he's inside for contempt of court; he simply won't talk about $1.4 million believed to be in offshore bank accounts. He's now been in prison longer than he would have if he'd just nicked the money.

Chadwick's lawyer has reported it as being 'like a sketch from *Monty Python*'.

Though we feel the Goons may be more accurate!

DID FERRIS BUELLER EVER DO THIS?

We've all done things we shouldn't have when we were growing up. However, the behaviour of two American boys really takes the biscuit. I say biscuit. What I mean is aeroplane.

The two teenage runaways – or should that be flyaways? – nicked their father's light aeroplane and flew for 90

minutes before crash landing. They're not badly hurt, but that's about as good as their situation gets.

Their stolen adventure happened in Big Bear City in California; it's thought the 14-year-olds were trying to get to Mexico but didn't have enough fuel. Both are now facing charges of theft.

There's only way to describe their behaviour. And that's plane stupid.

I WISH YOU'D NEVER BEEN BORN

A heartbreaking family story now, of two people stuck on opposite sides of the law.

Picture the scene. You're a policeman in Louistown, Illinois, who notices there is something familiar about the masked man caught on CCTV robbing a bank. As you study the footage, it becomes clear that the crook is your father – a respected former Marine who taught you right from wrong.

William Ginglen is now facing a life sentence because of his double life of armed robbery, drugs and prostitutes. His son, meanwhile, is probably thinking twice about the fatherly advice handed down to him over the years.

PACK OF LIES

Our next story is of an extremely thick villain. And when I say an extremely thick villain, I mean 36-stone of prime quality as-thick-as-a-milkshake thick.

The idiot in question, George Jolicoeur from Florida, has been busted for scamming fast-food restaurants into giving him free grub. As the *Daily Telegraph* reported, Mr Joliocoeur was accused of impersonating a policeman and then returning to the takeaways claiming to have found a hair in his food or shake. As a result, he then gets much more as compensation just to keep quiet.

George has been known to police for 15 years for various offences – of course, back then he was ten stone lighter so the following quote from the cops is priceless: 'We think he's consuming the food.'

I think they're right.

FUNFACT:

In Alaska, it is legal to shoot bears. However, waking a sleeping bear for the purpose of taking a photograph is prohibited.

SO NEAR AND YET SO FAR

What are the best places for a burglar to try and rob? A bank? A jeweller's? Whatever the answer, you're unlikely to find a police station towards the top of the list.

In Galveston in Texas, however, officers did not have far to go to arrest a burglar. The police found him *inside* the police station as he walked out with a taser-gun. Police also found the suspect in possession of a baton and an officer's mobile phone that he had just taken.

If only he'd stolen the cell key too – he might have had a chance of escaping when they banged him up.

A STASH COURSE IN STUPIDITY

You're a drug dealer. You've had your stash stolen. What are you going to do?

In Florida, two drugs dealers thought they had the answer. They phoned up the police to report the theft.

Ah.

The two dealers were promptly arrested.

DIAL M FOR MURDER, AND A FOR ARREST ...

To North Carolina where a man and his girlfriend – who thought they were dialling their local drug dealer – were arrested after dialling a police officer by mistake.

Mark Lewis inadvertently dialled Detective Rick Lynn's mobile, gave him his name and address and asked if he could bring them a rock of cocaine.

'That has to be one of the funniest things that's ever happened in my career,' Detective Rick said, summing the situation up perfectly.

YOU DOUGHNUT!

If you had two warrants out for your arrest would you get involved in a charity scavenger hunt requiring you to go into a police station? Thought not.

Well, one man in Michigan thought it was a great idea.

As part of the hunt, the man needed a photo of an officer eating a doughnut. Sounds easy enough, right?

Wrong. Instead, he was recognised from a 'Wanted' poster *on the wall in the police station* and was locked up.

Maybe we should set up a charity to help protect thick villains from their own stupid ideas ...

NOW YOU SEE IT ...

Drugs are bad for you and here's the proof.

52-year-old Anthony Martin from Illinois has become the latest person to call the police to complain that someone has stolen his illegal drugs. But there's more: Martin claimed a neighbour had taken his marijuana plants, but when he showed the officer the room where he usually kept them, the plants were still there.

Martin then argued that they must have been returned. Yep, that does seem the most likely explanation, doesn't it?

The police needed no further help with their enquiries!

A CHEEKY THICK VILLAIN

Some thick villains stories leave more questions unanswered than explained. Like this one ...

A naked man accused of trying to burgle a house in Cottonwood, Arizona, asked his victim for a pair of boxer shorts on his way out. Nickos Kopsaftis was arrested at the next house while apparently trying to steal a car.

The sheriff says he was wearing the shorts that were donated to him.

Yes, but why was he naked in the first place?

THE WAY THE LUCK FALLS

I've heard of some 'special' thick villains, but this one, you have to say, has been unlucky ...

A Nebraska man who jumped from a first-floor balcony, breaking a leg in the process, was arrested by the police he was trying to evade ... but they weren't even looking for him.

Police say they went to an apartment looking for a suspect in a recent burglary. When no one answered the door, the deputies turned to leave, then heard a thud.

It wasn't the burglary suspect they were seeking. Nonetheless, he was arrested on outstanding theft warrants.

LAUGHING ALL THE WAY TO THE BANK

At some point this dad must have thought he'd made a mistake but, it seems, he ploughed on regardless ...

Michael Lyons thought he'd come up with a great practical joke for his daughter's birthday party – but he stopped laughing as soon as he was arrested.

As he stopped by a bank with the party guests in the US state of Georgia, he convinced one of his daughter's 13-year-old pals to hand a note to a cashier, stating 'Give me all of your money, this is a stick-up.' The cashier sounded the alarm and cops stormed the building.

Happy birthday dear daughter, happy birth ... clink.

SILLY BANKER

Here's a tip for bank robbers: if you're going to hold up a branch, don't hold up the one that you use yourself.

That's what's happened in Tennessee where a robber who held up a bank was recognised as a regular customer by staff. A cashier clocked Michael Rush, *who has an account at the branch*, when he tried to hold it up.

Cashiers were also able to tell police what sort of car Rush drove when he visits the bank.

They weren't, however, able to tell them why Rush had been so stupid as to rob somewhere where everyone knew him.

RETURN TO SENDER

Sometimes, you *almost* feel sorry for thick villains. Take the following story, where the trust in the victim is almost touching.

Two robbers in Utah have been caught after they agreed to return a stolen mobile phone in exchange for $300. The victim had sent a text to his phone saying `I really want my phone back. I'll pay you the money for the phone right now.'

He got a reply that said: 'OK, let's do this.'

They arranged to meet up and, of course, so did the police.

PRIZE IDIOT

SORRY I ROBBED YOU, WILL YOU GO OUT WITH ME?
Never mix business with pleasure, goes the maxim. And if your business is robbery, it's one maxim that you would do very well to remember.

In Delaware, USA, a man who robbed a pizza delivery girl has been captured after he asked his victim for a date. Police say that Brent Brown called his 18-year-old victim on his mobile phone to apologise and propose a date.

She declined but gave the number to police. We're guessing Brent might be off the dating scene for a while.

CLASS IDIOTS

It's the latent school teacher in me who enjoys all those convictions secured because of terrible spelling.

If only these boys, and it is mainly boys, had paid a little more attention in class, maybe they wouldn't have ended up in the clink dreading shower time.

TIME FOR A SPELL IN PRISON

Different criminals have developed different calling cards over the years – from graffiti tags to horses' heads. But Preston's 27-year-old Lee Wilson is perhaps unique in developing his moniker – an inability to spell.

Wilson caused £11,000 worth of damage to his ex's car. The finishing touch, however, was spraying the word – and I use the word 'word' loosely – B-I-C-H across it. When Wilson repeated the misspelling in a text message, the police had their man

Wilson has subsequently been jaled, sorry, jailed.

DOCTOR, I'VE GOT A BAD CASE OF BEING STUPID

Memo to thick villains: before you assume someone else's identity, it's always best to do a little basic research first.

A court heard recently how 27-year-old James Burnett from Norfolk wanted to get out of a meeting with his probation officers. James thought he'd cracked it when he came up with the following cunning plan. He found a hospital appointment letter and changed the recipient from 'Mrs' to 'Mr'.

What could possibly go wrong?

Well, what went wrong was that the appointment was with a gynaecologist.

Oops.

IS IT A BOY? IS IT A GIRL? NO, IT'S AN IDIOT

You might think James Burnett might be the only man with gynaecological problems. Well, you'd be wrong.

Take the man in South Africa who claimed *he was* pregnant and needed a week off work. Charles Sibindana, not the sharpest knife in the drawer, used a medical certificate stolen from a health centre – apparently unaware only women require gynaecologists.

Charles has been fined the equivalent of £72 by magistrates in Vereeniging, though his stupidity was priceless.

A POOR COPY OF A REAL VILLAIN

One of the basic rules about being a criminal has to be this: don't leave behind any clues as to who the perpetrator might be.

This priceless knowledge has not quite been passed down to our thick villain friends, or Bandido Grosso, in Mexico. Vandals who broke into a school over the Christmas holidays were thoughtful enough to leave behind a photocopied mugshot of one of their gang.

Headmistress Maria del Rosario Gomes said, 'It's the third time the school has been vandalised but now we have got a very good idea who did it!'

I guess one should be grateful it was only their mugshots they left behind.

TATTOO DUMB FOR WORDS

In Japan, the 'Yakuza' mafia are recognisable by the blue tattoos they have hidden on their bodies. I wonder what the equivalent thick villain signature would be ...?

One possible answer can be found in Detroit, USA where bank robber Andrew Webster was arrested after witnesses identified him ... thanks to his tattoo.

What was it about the tattoo that made it so recognisable you ask? Perhaps it was the fact that Webster has the word DUMB written on his skin ...

There's not much more that one can add to that, is there?

PRIZE IDIOT

MY NAME IS ... CECIL

Here's another piece of advice for any thick villains out there: if you've got your name tattooed on a prominent part of your body, you might want to think carefully before taking up crime as a vocation.

Take the man from Indiana who gave local police officers a wrong name after being stopped for a driving offence. He was caught out though after they noticed his real name tattooed on his neck. 25-year-old Cecil Carmer told officers his name was Robert, even though they could see CECIL etched in large letters across his skin.

Perhaps if Cecil had been quick-witted, he might have been able to bluff that his name was Robert Cecil, or even Cecil Robert. But being quick witted is one thing thick villains are not, so he owned up.

Cecil awaits trial.

FASHION POLICE

The hoodie, the baseball cap and the tracksuit are *de rigueur* these days for petty criminals and ASBOs loitering outside a grotty corner shop.

But some thick villains just don't seem to want to blend into the background; it's as if they positively enjoy dressing up for the occasion and want to get caught!

'Now try on these standard-issue prison clothes ... they are so hot right now!'

ANYTHING THAT MARKED THE BANK ROBBER OUT? WHERE DO YOU WANT ME TO START?

Subtle. Inconspicuous. Difficult to spot. A master of disguise. These are just some of the terms that can't really be levelled at our next criminal *incompetent*.

Not so much a thick villain as a thickly made-up villain, this robber in Australia entered a bank brandishing a gun ... and wearing a dress and roller blades. Dubbed the 'Mrs Doubtfire Bandit', he demanded money and then rolled into the street at high speed.

Witnesses say the robber wore a striking white dress with a floral pattern and a pair of leggings. The look was completed by a black wig with a blue stripe.

Whatever happened to the good old trusty balaclava?

I guess they are just *so* last year!

WHAT NOT TO WEAR. EVER.

There's confident. And there's brazen. And then there is just downright stupid.

Burgled Bedford shopkeeper and clothes designer Neil Primett reported how he was stunned to see a man pass by his shop fully dressed in his not-yet-unveiled new designs – particularly as they all clashed when put together.

The passer-by was caught with his pants down when he was spotted wearing green check trousers with a tracksuit top *and* (if that wasn't bad enough) an electric-blue sleeveless T-shirt with the word 'CRIMINAL' in luminous yellow emblazoned across it.

As the *Guardian* reported, the very thick villain was taken away in a car with one word emblazoned on it too – POLICE.

It's unclear whether he'll also be charged for crimes against fashion, but we all agree he should.

NOT QUITE MODEL BEHAVIOUR

Most thieves in clothes shops are after, well, the clothes. But this particular robber had his eyes on something else entirely ...

The thief, who has what can only be described as a fetish for 'female mannequins', has been jailed for repeatedly breaking into shops. 39-year-old Ron Dotson lives with his parents (obviously) in Detroit and was arrested in October, shortly after being paroled for his sixth conviction in thirteen years.

Police spotted him near a smashed shop window that had a mannequin wearing a French maid's outfit on display. Police later found him in an alleyway escaping with three mannequins dressed in lingerie ... possibly looking forward to a quiet evening in. It was not to be.

Of course there's a technical term for a mannequin thief – they're known as dummies.

THE CHEEK OF IT ALL

Meet a man whose calling card is somewhat bizarre ...

Nebraskan Christopher Willever has made a name for himself as the 'bare-bottomed bandit' and has been regularly caught on CCTV crawling around a shop with his pants down. Detectives received a tip-off from someone who had seen the tape of a man flashing his flesh for up to four minutes as he shuffled around the floor of the Tobacco Hut.

One cop wittily remarked, 'I guess somebody recognised either end of him.'

THONGS OF PRAISE!

A story which combines a thick villain with a thong ... what could be better?

In Kentucky, police were able to track down a burglar (or should that be bunglar!) after he dropped a video camera of himself actually committing the crime. Though ridiculous that isn't the strange part of the story. Idiot Rodney McMillen, who was eventually disturbed by the resident he was robbing, was dressed only in a green thong. In the rush to flee the scene McMillen left behind the video camera, which also included his footage of a family party.

Yes, I'm wondering too why he was only wearing a green thong. But I guess it's fair to say that in terms of this guy being a criminal, he was a bit pants.

BEING BAD. LOOKING GOOD ...

With some crimes, it can take weeks of police investigating to work out the one piece of identification or evidence that will help nail the criminal. With other crimes, it's more a question of just how many distinguishing marks will stand out the most.

Take the following case in Monterey, California, where a bearded man in full drag has been arrested after robbing a petrol station. Armed man Michael Clouse was wearing a black evening gown, fishnet stockings, calf-high boots and a black wig, and had stuffed $400 in cash into a matching black handbag.

So, which of these many features was the criminal's undoing? If you guessed the fishnet tights, award yourself a pat on the back. The robber was arrested after police spotted a car with a fishnet stocking dragging along the ground from the driver's door.

I wonder if the thief is hoping for a suspender-ed sentence?

PRIZE IDIOT

MEMO:

FAO: Thick Villains

RE: Always match your disguise to the weather conditions.

Two armed robbers were jailed recently for wearing winter jackets and woolly hats on *one of the hottest days of the year*.

Carl Cook and Chris Jones wanted to rob a landlord of his takings in Bournemouth, but were forced to hang around for five hours in 100 degree heat before getting him. Many locals had already noted down their suspicious details.

Doesn't their stupidity make you get all hot under the collar?

DRUNK AND DISORGANISED

Kids, getting hammered is not big and it's not clever ... even if it is bloody good fun.

We've all done stupid things while intoxicated but most of us don't go-a-burglaring. The following sad saps may have needed Dutch courage to go stealing and plundering but a quiet pint soon turned into nine loud ones.

For example, how drunk do you have to be to think that holding up a petrol station with a tennis racquet is a good idea?
New balls please ...

SLEEPING ON THE JOB

Some thick villains are just a bit too cheeky for their own good ...

In California, a nude man broke into a woman's house and was caught after having fallen asleep on her sofa. Michael Bonnie was promptly arrested for not only attempted burglary but indecent exposure as well.

It can't be a good thing to be a naked thief, can it? You must be leaving all sorts of prints all over the place.

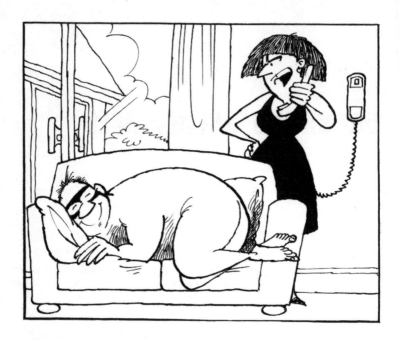

FLUSH GORDON

Have you ever visited a pub, visited their loos and been so impressed with the set-up, you decided to take them home with you?

No, neither have I. But that's exactly what happened at the Royal Oak pub in Southampton, where a 42-year-old decided to take a urinal home with him as 'a souvenir'. *A urinal!* Quite how he smuggled the urinal out is unclear – let's only hope he didn't try to hide it under his jumper.

Later on, presumably after having sobered up, the man handed himself and the urinal in to a local police station and was cautioned. Which in a way is a shame, as I like the thought of the police searching for their number one suspect ...

I FOUGHT THE SNORE ... AND THE SNORE WON

What is it with burglars falling asleep on the job? If you're on the nightshift, at least make sure you've had enough kip (or coffee) to keep you awake during the robbery.

Otherwise, you'll end up like American burglar Ian Wright, who was caught after falling asleep in a basement of a home he decided to rob.

Police found Mr Wright snoring away next to his packed 'swag' bag full of stereo equipment, a backpack and a wallet. Fair play to him for giving it a go, though: the rubbish robber told the police in Missoula, Montana, that he was drunk and had passed out after a party at the home.

There was just one problem: the homeowners hadn't been hosting a party.

It's not all bad – at least he'll be able to catch up on some sleep in the cells.

YOU CANNOT BE SERIOUS

If you were planning on holding up a petrol station, what might you consider taking with you as a weapon? A gun? A baseball bat? Sadly, nothing so straightforward was used by our next thick villain, whose weapon of choice was a, um, tennis racquet.

To be fair, 20-year-old Ernesto Martinez did tell the petrol station that he was armed with an Uzi machine gun. However, it was game, set and match when he was 'disarmed' by a security guard, and his actual weapon was revealed.

Among other things Martinez was arrested on suspicion of being under the influence of a controlled substance, which makes more sense when considering what he was trying to pull off. Or maybe he and Roger Federer had one of those embarrassing bag switches. In which case, be careful if you've got front row seats at Wimbledon ...

ICH BIN EIN BERLINER

John F Kennedy once famously declared, 'Ich bin ein Berliner', thinking he'd said 'I am a Berliner', whereas, in fact, he'd declared 'I am a doughnut'. Our next thick villain is very much a 'Berliner' in both senses of the word.

When a Berlin cyclist rode into a lamp post whilst drunk, he was too embarrassed to tell his wife what happened. So instead of telling his partner the truth, he went and told the police a pack of lies instead. Not a smart move.

The cyclist told officers that two men had attempted to mug him, but that he had managed to valiantly beat them off. All of this was going smoothly until he pointed out the bushes where the muggers had fled from. The bushes contained a wire fence that was pretty much impassable. A bit like the story he was trying to spin.

WHO'S BEEN SLEEPING IN MY BED?

In the children's story 'Goldilocks and the Three Bears', Goldilocks shamelessly trespasses into the bears' house, and greedily steals their porridge before rounding off her visit by falling asleep in their bed.

Our next story from Gloucestershire follows a similar narrative, except that rather than finding Goldilocks under his duvet, Shane Williams returned home from the pub to find a drunken burglar also stealing forty winks in his bed. Sadly, this winker did not get his oats though. The burglar, who'd been ransacking the flat, fled the scene, only to be caught an hour later.

It wasn't the burglar's first misdemeanour of the night. Bizarrely, our real life Goldilocks had been chucked out of the *same* pub Shane Williams had been drinking in earlier in the evening.

Time for a spot of porridge, I think.

IT'S A FAIR KIP

How many times do I have to tell thick villains? Don't kip on the job.

A burglar who targeted an off-licence in Thailand has been caught. I say 'caught' though that tends to imply that the villain was a moving target.

Police say the robber-to-be downed a few beers during the raid and was found snoring under the owner's bed.

Not so much a 'Tiger' or 'Cobra', more of a bit of a lemming. The villain now faces a six-month jail sentence.

THE WASSOCK OF OZ

Not quite a thick villain in this story but I think he squeezes into the category purely based on his sheer stupidity ...

A drunk driver in Australia stopped a police car to ask for directions to Ayers Rock ... just 100 yards from the massive landmark. The *Daily Telegraph* reported his headlights were even shining on the 348m orange monolith, also known as Uluru. A case of the headlights were on, but no-one was home?

The driver now faces charges for being over his legal limit of idiocy.

OH, WHAT A NIGHT!

This next thick villain had what is best described as a night-and-a-half to remember. Or possibly a night-and-a-half to forget.

The man in the American state of Delaware was arrested shortly after being rescued from a muddy swamp. What was he doing in the swamp in the first place? Apparently, he'd had an argument with a prostitute in a field and then got lost trying to find his way home. Police claimed he called for help on his mobile before being tugged free by a rescue helicopter.

The man faces several charges including solicitation, trespassing and being stupid.

HO, HO, HO

What could warm the heart more than to combine Yuletide joy with a thick-villain story ...

We go to the Square Mile where a well-known 'tea leaf' got slightly more than he bargained for after wandering into the staff Christmas do for, wait for it .... the City of London police force.

It's difficult to know who was more surprised. The thief recognised most of the people in the bar – and most of the people in the bar recognised him. At which point, the festivities were put to one side: the thief scarpered and the police put out a radio call. The man was arrested shortly afterwards in possession of credit cards nicked from another pub.

Deck the cells with bells and holly ... ha ha ha ha ha ha ha ha ha!

ONE IDIOT TO GO PLEASE, WITH EXTRA IDIOCY

Hannibal Lecter from *The Silence of the Lambs* is well known for his love of Chianti. But the infamous character also knew when to enjoy a glass of the Italian wine, and when it was time to 'work'.

Unlike our next 'villain'.

The 51 year-old burglar from Stockport raided an Italian restaurant, but drank so much of their Chianti his illegal raid ended with him attempting to use the chip and pin machine *to phone a friend*, before passing out on the floor.

The dough ball's been jailed for four months.

DUMB RAIDER

An open letter to thick villains everywhere: if you're robbing someone's house, don't make yourself at home and start playing their video games. And if you really must do so, try to not fall asleep while playing them.

But that's what happened at a house in Wales, when homeowner Grace Hodges came downstairs to discover the burglar fast asleep on her sofa. At first, she thought it must be a friend of her daughter's. When her daughter didn't recognise him, they called the police.

I think that's what is known as G-A-M-E-O-V-E-R.

THREE-POINT TWERP

Not so much a thick villain here as a very, very thick driving student ...

In Germany, a young man has failed his driving exam because he turned up to the test *three times* over the legal limit. The examiner smelt the booze straight away and directed the man to what turned out to be an 'emergency stop' at the police station in Bendorf.

What I want to know is this: can you lose your licence if you haven't actually got it yet?

PRIZE IDIOT

WHAT GOES AROUND

This next story has all the right ingredients for a classic thick villain tale: a Welsh port, two Irishmen who'd missed their ferry and quite a lot of booze.

If you or I had missed our ferry, we might consider heading back to the pub or finding somewhere to sleep for the night. But such logic was not so apparent for our intrepid heroes. Instead, they hatched a cunning plan to get back to Dublin and stole a trawler from Holyhead.

I say 'cunning'. Sadly, for them, their nautical skills were, well, nought. Having motored round in circles for two hours, their 'booze cruise' was over and they embarrassingly sent out a Mayday call to be rescued.

INCOMPETENCE ALERT!

What could be grander than a collection of cretins? People who are so stupid and so off their heads (sometimes both) that they think selling drugs to a uniformed copper or turning up for a bank heist after closing time is acceptable behaviour for supposed criminals. It's not.

These people aren't putting in the most basic level of research and so deserve our utter contempt.

Get a proper job, son.

THERE'S BEING IDENTIFIABLE BY DENTAL RECORDS, AND THERE'S ...

How do you identify a criminal from the clues they have left behind? Sometimes all forensics have to work with is a fingerprint, a strand of hair, or a fragment of clothing. And sometimes, as in the case of this next thick villain, a slightly bigger clue is left behind.

Polish police were hunting a man who broke into a car, when they discovered a more useful clue left behind – a set of false teeth.

Officers used dental records to track down 54-year-old Voitek Lekovski who admitted they were his dentures. Voitek said to police, in a rather gummy accent I presume: 'Yes, they are mine but I don't know how they got there, they were stolen from me.'

Police deliberated for a moment before thinking Voitek's story was as false as his teeth, and he has been charged with wobbery, sorry, robbery.

DON'T MOVE – I'VE GOT A GUM!

Not so much a story about a thick criminal mastermind here, as a tale about a gummy villain in a hurry.

Police in Sweden have used dental records to trace a thief after he left his false teeth at the scene of the crime. It wasn't a difficult job to track the villain down – his teeth had his social-security number engraved upon them.

When the man was arrested, he told the police, 'I ran off because I couldn't find anything worth nicking.'

It's like pulling teeth with thick villains, isn't it?

ANOTHER CASE WITH BITE

When burgling, it's best to avoid leaving very definite clues to your identity and, to my knowledge, this is the third such case in recent years: a thick villain leaving behind his false teeth.

To Hartlepool where William Sowerby has been given a suspended prison sentence. His dentures were found in the bedroom of a flat he broke into. Sowerby had denied theft even when police caught him with a camcorder from the flat. Teesside Crown Court heard he only gave in when confronted with his gnashers.

Detective Inspector Keith Groves said: 'Officers asked the homeowner if the false teeth were theirs and they weren't. That's how we were able to link him to the crime. It's very rare that a burglar leaves behind this kind of clue.'

I guess he'd bitten off more than he could chew.

IN THICKNESS AND IN HEALTH

Of course, thick villains get married too. It's just that they do things differently to the rest of us. As in this story from Dorchester, where the words 'Happiest Day of My Life' probably didn't occur to this feeble fiancée, or probably his furious wife-to-be.

28-year-old Simon Hooper wanted to propose to his girlfriend the good old-fashioned way. However, rather than the age-old tradition of actually paying for the diamond ring, he employed the slightly more unorthodox tactic of swallowing the £1700 piece when the jeweller turned his back. Hooper was then held in police cells for three days until the ring 're-emerged'.

He's since been jailed for 12 weeks

In his case, I guess the old adage is true: marriage isn't a word, it's a sentence.

UNTIL THEFT DO US PART

Simon Hooper (the ring pooper, *from overleaf*) isn't the only young romantic looking for different ways to pay for his wedding. Take this next couple, whose plans for their big day included the limo, the meal, the table plan, the holiday ... and the bank robbery.

While the rest of us try to work out just how we're going to afford everything, the couple in Lindon, Utah robbed the Wells Fargo bank three times to pay for their wedding and honeymoon.

Talk about something borrowed ...

CREDIT WHERE CREDIT'S DUE

The following thick villain has been foiled thanks to some really bad luck – not that he deserved any luck whatsoever ...

In Oslo, Norway, pizza deliveryman Vegard Sjaastad recognised the credit card he was given as payment – chiefly because it was his. It had been stolen the day before. Vegard completed the delivery, told the man to enjoy the pizza and then called the police.

I think that's what's known as an extra-topping of hard cheese.

THE DRIVER'S NOT FOR TURNING

Fast forward now to a criminal idiot who is more than a little backwards ...

Police in Australia have charged a driver with a rather interesting motoring offence – 'reversing further than necessary'. That might sound a little bit harsh. What next? Parking too far from the kerb? Honking in an urban area? But you haven't heard how far the driver reversed up – more than 30 miles along one of the country's busiest roads.

Police say the driver was stopped on the Hume Highway – which runs between Sydney and Melbourne. The man still had 50 miles to go to his hometown of Numurkah and claimed reverse was the only gear that worked.

An unfair punishment? I'm staying neutral on that one.

COINING IT IN ... ALMOST

If you're a hay-fever sufferer, you probably shouldn't get a job in a flower shop. And if you're wannabe villain, you probably should seek employment at the Royal Mint, unless you're planning for a long stint in jail.

Our man in the Royal Australian Mint had worked out a way of smuggling the coins out – in his boots and his lunch box. The problem was getting rid of the 100,000 shiny new coins. A supermarket rejected his piles of pristine coins and when he tried to exchange a large quantity of coins at a pub, the police were brought in.

He's now in jail, taking notes on how to be a better citizen.

SILENCING THE PRESS – THICK-VILLAIN STYLE

As thick villains stories go, this Chinese takeaway mystery is a bit of a prawn cracker.

A diner at a Chinese restaurant in Weston-super-Mare bit off more than he could chew when he discovered a cockroach among his king prawns. The restaurant was duly fined £20,000.

So far, so revolting. But what happened next was that the restaurant tried to hush up the court case to spectacularly bad effect. Their plan was simple – to stop people reading the story in the local newspaper, they'd just buy up every copy they could find. Which they did – all 1400 copies sold out in two hours after two men went round bulk buying from every newsagent within 20 miles.

Backfired though, didn't it? Not only is all of Somerset

talking about the restaurant but the story has been on radio, and is now in this book for posterity.

For bookings please call 01934 ...

OUR NEXT CALLER IS THICK FROM CHICAGO ...

Dear thick villains,

Thanks for being so entertaining but if you rob a bank, it's best not to call up a radio show afterwards and boast about what you've just done. It's just silly isn't it?

Well, that's what happened in Chicago where a bank robber was arrested after phoning a radio station and boasting of his achievements. Of all the dumb things to do, Randy Washington proudly claimed how he and five others carried out the crime with inside help from an employee.

The radio station gave his mobile-phone number to the FBI.

FYI FBI ... he did it.

THE WRONG BAG LADY TO ROB

I don't know whether this villain is thick, or just plain unlucky.

An escaped convict's been caught – after he tried to steal the handbag of an off-duty policewoman. The 34-year-old Belgian, who'd been on the run for a month, attempted the theft just a few blocks from a Brussels police station.

A second off-duty officer arrested him.

I think that's what known as bags to rights.

HI JACK, ER, HELLO OFFICER

It had all been going so well for our next pair of thick villains. Until, that is, they tried to make their getaway.

The villains in question had stolen £7000 in takings from a bowling alley in Bishop's Stortford and would have got away with it had it not been for their decision to choose the wrong getaway vehicle: the car they tried to hijack contained two plain-clothed police officers ...

Strike!

YOU'VE GOT TO HAND IT TO THE POLICE

You've got a load of stolen goods. You need a hand in carrying them. Who's the best person to ask? Probably not a policeman ...

In Wandsworth, 28-year-old Bryan O'Gorman was arrested after asking a London bobby to help him carry stolen goods over a fence. The PC was off-duty at the time. But not for long. O'Gorman had no choice but to plead guilty.

I don't know whether he asked for other fences to be taken into consideration.

TOUR DE FARCE

Off we go to Barnstaple for our next thick thief, who made the elementary error of showing off what he'd stolen.

The deviant 'mastermind' stole a bicycle from a police

station. Surprisingly, he then thought it would be a good idea to flaunt his theft by riding the bike past the coppers a few days later. Unsurprisingly, he was nicked.

The only handlebars he'll be handling from now on are his cell bars.

PRIZE IDIOT

I *almost* feel sorry for our next stupid shoplifter, as she was the victim of a store's cunning plan to trap her for repeated stealing.

The New Zealand, Winona Ryder-wannabe in question was caught after a store duped her into believing she'd won a prize. The shop put up an image of the thief taken by CCTV cameras under the heading 'Lucky Shopper' to entice thief Amy Adams back into the store. Ms Adams was arrested when she asked to claim her prize.

She got a pair of handcuffs, which was nice.

LEAF IT OUT, OFFICER

Sometimes in life, things just land in your lap. That was the case for the Croatian police force, on the hunt for a burglar.

The Police officers hunting the thief had their job made a lot easier when the escapee fell like a gift from the heavens. Well, a tree to be precise. The thief had attempted to flee from a recently burgled house in Zagreb by climbing down a tree, but fell from the branches right in front of the coppers.

Not exactly a case for special branch.

AN OPEN AND SHUT CASE

Time for another memo to thick villains: if you're going to rob a bank, make sure you check the opening hours before you plan your raid.

This Croatian bank robber was left empty-handed, and red faced, after turning up ten minutes after the bank had shut. Staff at the Podravska Bank in Zagreb claimed they heard the entrance doors rattling and a masked man holding a gun trying to get in. Bank workers claimed he eventually walked off looking very confused.

Not so much overdraft as over daft.

COURT IN THE ACT

You're up in court. You've got some drugs on you. Who can you trust to look after them during the hearing? There's a certain logic to the thoughts of our next scoundrel, you've got to admit. Logical *and* thick.

In Wigan, a 20-year-old dude was due in court before The Man for breaking the terms of his parole. But he made things much worse for himself by asking the court's *security staff* to look after *his drugs*. The bemused staff offered him a receipt to sign and the court proceeded.

The man was later fined £50 for possession. Though, to be honest, that should be the least of his problems.

GOD ARREST YE MERRY GENTLEMEN

Carol singers might not always be the most welcome of visitors, but at the least the worst you can normally expect is a tuneless rendition of some yuletide classic. What you don't expect is for carol singers to spray you with CS gas ...

That's what happened in Weymouth, where police carried out a drugs raid disguised as, wait for it, Victorian carol singers. A nine-strong team of burly officers armed with a sniffer dog were dressed in cloaks and top hats with a Christmas lantern, as well as the standard-issue, stab-proof vests and CS gas.

When the occupants opened up the door, the team announced their true identity and seized a stash of cocaine worth £400.

'... and a happy five years.'

FEATHERING HIS NEST

Ridiculous rogues don't always think about the best clothing to wear before they step out to steal other people's stuff.

In Germany, a thief wearing a bizarre quilted jacket snagged it while stealing from the shop he was in and then left a trail of feathers all the way home. He had nicked a karaoke machine – all the police had to do was follow the feathery trail Hansel and Gretel style.

Though, how a man in a quilt nicking a karaoke machine wasn't spotted in the first place I'll never know.

THERE'S NO PLACE LIKE HOME

Homing pigeons. It's a simple enough concept. Not simple enough, it seems, for our next thick villain.

The pigeons in question were stolen from a loft in Cambridgeshire. However, they soon outfoxed their captors – by simply flying home. Pigeon owner Philip Pearce says his racing birds were back within days of being snatched, claiming, 'Whoever took them obviously didn't know much about homing pigeons.'

Not much of a criminal coo.

A CROC OF LIES

Our next dimwit is more of a thick benefits cheat. But I'll allow it ...

A 53-year-old from Eccles claimed he was unable to walk but was recently rumbled when investigators found a holiday snap of him wrestling an alligator in Florida. He'd banked more than £17,000 in benefits and was also running a pirate DVD market stall. Oh, and he'd also achieved a black belt in ju jitsu.

Should come in handy for where he's going next. The man has been sentenced to 12 months behind bars.

GOOD COP, BAD COP

This next story involves a policeman in Sweden who's turned bad.

He's admitted to carrying out an armed robbery in Stockholm and then investigating it in a bid to hush it up. Colleagues became suspicious when he bought a new car with crisp banknotes.

Turns out they were Abba-solutely right.

MASS ARREST

In Rome a man wanted by police tried to escape by running into a church – only to find it filled with officers attending Mass.

Gilberto Carnoale had cunningly escaped house arrest but, to his utter bad luck, officers attending the service recognised him. However, before they hauled him away, they allowed him to join in the rest of the Mass.

I wonder if he also went to confession?

IS IT 'COS I IS THICK?

... and now over to a thick villain from Birmingham who, unbelievably, modelled himself on Ali G.

The *Sun* reported how a cocky 22-year-old wannabe dressed up as Ali G to ambush cash-delivery trucks, openly used stolen bank notes with security dye all over them and, and this is the real clanger, left a picture of the haul on his mobile phone.

Big up yaself ... idiot.

A BIRD IN THE HAND IS WORTH TWO IN THE NICK

In more feather-related fun, Monty, an African Grey parrot was recently taken hostage for fear he would grass on burglar David Carlisle. Monty, had 'witnessed' Carlisle during the raid in Wiltshire and when police arrested the bumbling thief, Carlisle was reported to have said 'Parrots can talk and I didn't want it grassing me up!'

Monty was sold and remains at large. Carlisle, meanwhile, has all the time in the world to figure out just how stupid he is. In his cell.

THE HITMAN AND HER

My latest thick villain story takes us to Tokyo and it involves a love triangle. It's complicated, so read carefully ...

A woman wanted her lover's wife to be murdered so much

she hired an assassin. After six months the wife was still alive so she complained to the police when the hitman didn't do the job. Lover Eriko Kawaguchi reportedly paid the would-be shooter £75,000.

Kawaguchi is now wishing she hadn't brought the whole 'attempted murder' nonsense up.

POINTING THE FINGER

Police are used to dusting for fingerprints but less used to finding the actual finger. A careless burglar in Hildesheim, Germany left behind the vital clue after catching his hand on the broken glass.

Police matched the finger very quickly to some prints they had on file. The suspect initially denied it was his until detectives produced the original.

When it comes to pointing the finger of blame, it doesn't come more simple than that, does it?

NOT SO FLASH

Winners don't do drugs. Well, this weiner clearly does ...

A flasher has been jailed after claiming he wasn't exposing himself – he was merely holding a jumbo hot dog under his coat. The 61-year-old man from Guernsey claimed in court that he was innocent allhough strangely he couldn't resist boasting that the fictional hot dog was jumbo-sized.

THIS IS A ... HEY! WHERE DID EVERYONE GO?

When a team of bank robbers broke into a bank's headquarters in Constanta, Romania, they received a somewhat dispiriting sight.

The building was empty. The bank had moved a week prior.

Maybe next time, lads ...

PINKY AND NOT SO PERKY

The future of penal reform is bright, the future is ... pink.

A county jail in Texas claims it's had a dramatic impact on the number of reoffenders, simply by giving inmates pink jumpsuits and slippers.

The sheriff of Mason County, Clint Low, says local criminals hate the new fatigues and re-offending rates are down 70 per cent.

FUNFACT:

In Zion, Illinois, it is illegal for anyone to give cats or dogs, or other domesticated animals, a lighted cigar.

PRIZE IDIOT

BAD DEAL

A drug dealer in Florida has been arrested after he offered to sell crack.

To a uniformed police officer.

Sat in a marked police car.

Michael Garibay walked up to Deputy Sheriff Ed Johnson at a petrol station and asked: 'Do you want to buy some crack?' Thinking he was joking, Johnson said 'Yes', at which point Garibay pulled out a plastic bag containing cocaine.

Do not pass go.

Do not collect £200.

Go straight to jail ...

GRAND THEFT IDIOT

Imagine you're a bank robber. Imagine having planned the most cunning heist ever ... only for you to have forgotten to fill the getaway car with any petrol. Imagine your embarrassment at trying to explain that in court.

However, if you are a thick villain these schoolboy errors happen more commonly than you think.

For any thick villains reading, I hope you are taking notes ...

THE NOT SO GREAT ESCAPE

An Exeter prisoner's jailbreak was thwarted lately, somewhat clumsily, when he tripped on his shoelaces and fell 30ft from a hole in his cell wall.

After toiling impressively for two hours with *only a dustpan and brush* from his third-floor cell, Darren Humphreys had dug his way through five layers of bricks and mortar.

Having tied his bed sheets together, the 40-year-old drug dealer then attempted to climb down to the prison courtyard below. Although things didn't quite go to plan when he tripped on his shoelaces and stumbled out the cell ... breaking his ankle in the process. The guards heard him scream and captured him though he hadn't exactly got far.

Eat your heart out, Steve McQueen!

HOW NOT TO LEG IT

A burglar in California has been caught red-handed after he was let down by his artificial leg.

Police in Pomona captured Gregory Daniels after his prosthetic leg fell off as he attempted to flee after trying to steal a cash machine using a pick-up truck, reports the *Metro* newspaper. As the 48-year-old leapt out of the truck to flee on foot, his false leg fell off, stopping him in his tracks.

That's what I call a fair hop.

THE TRUTH, THE HOLE TRUTH ...

In a scene reminiscent of an Ealing comedy, Stephen Brady was caught breaking in to an off-licence by cutting a hole through the floor of the room above. As Brady slid down through the hole, the alarm went off. Panicking, the bungling burglar slipped and became wedged in the hole ... head-first!

It took fire crews an hour to free him after using him, no doubt, as a human piñata.

Brady was given four months in jail to get his head together.

THE CURIOUS CASE OF THE LOAN GUNMAN

Its not often you get customer service with a smile ... or by a man robbing the bank.

A bank thief in Austria decided to take calls from customers while surrounded by police for five hours.

Armed officers surrounded the bank in Vienna minutes after Guenther Baum stormed in with a gun demanding money. Rather than give up straight away though, the dopey villain took calls from customers and began offering them discounts on loans and services.

When he finally gave himself up, bank staff had to deal with the angry customers who thought they had secured a great deal on their loans.

IF ONLY IT HAD BEEN GREEN

A police chase in New Hampshire came to an unexpected end, when the fleeing felon stopped at red lights.

24-year-old Joshua Grant led police on a chase through three towns and although spike strips that popped his tyres could not stop him, a simple traffic light did.

A bemused police spokesman said, 'It was pretty simple to box him in.'

Sounds like another simple case of the lights were on, but nobody was home ...

SHAFTED

Despite all evidence to the contrary, my thick villains are still trying to use air vents to break-in ... and get out.

In New York, a man has been found stuck in the casing of an air conditioner – his head and arms were sticking outside with the rest of his body inside the grocery store. His pockets were jammed with cash from the till. Sadly for him he was jammed in the vent.

Remember, this only works in the movies!

CHIM CHIMEREE

We all know that Father Christmas makes his way into people's homes by going down the chimney to deliver presents. Our next thick villain followed Santa's modus operandi ... though he was very much into taking rather than giving.

Just one problem: this in-the-buff burglar (yes, he was naked) got stuck on the way down. San Francisco police claimed the 23-year-old had locked himself out. It's not a complete surprise to discover he was also charged for being under the influence of drugs.

Potty behaviour, in every sense of the word.

SHAFTED: THE SEQUEL

With a surname befitting his behaviour, Gary Burke broke into a Woolworths in Brighton and nicked two mobile phones. On his way out, Burke tripped the alarm and then tried to escape through the air vent.

Burke was found by police with just his head sticking out.

Talk about being caught upto your neck in it.

BY GORGE, THEY'VE BLOWN IT

To Bristol for some thick villains who really hadn't thought through their escape plan ...

The burglars, on-the-run from a suspected burglary, had to be saved by mountain rescue after trying to climb down Avon Gorge – a 250ft cliff. A police helicopter eventually spotted the buffoons after they had become stuck on a ledge.

I suspect the prison guards won't have any problems with them trying to scale the walls to escape anytime in the near future.

ROW DEAR

Two robbers in Norway thought a rowing boat would be the perfect getaway vehicle after they ransacked another boat.

One problem: they couldn't row.

Police in Askvoll reported it wasn't hard to catch up with the pair as they were rowing in opposite directions and going round in circles.

Simply oarful.

AW-FUEL

Balaclava.

Check.

Black outfit.

Check.

Swag bag.

Check.

Getaway car fuelled up.

Er, hang on ...

A thick villain has been arrested in Romania after he grabbed £20,000 from a shop before leaping into his getaway car ... which he had forgetten to fill up.

He was caught red-handed. And red-faced too, presumably.

KARMA?

A bank robber in Athens was shot dead by his accomplice after a botched burglary. After a bank employee had tried to stop the pair fleeing, one of the robbers started shooting aimlessly. Amidst the gunfire, the robber accidently shot his partner-in-crime.

GETAWAY KARMA?

Ever had a bad day at the office? Well, I bet it's not as bad as this thick villain's ...

A thief in Milwaukee must have thought the robbery was going well – the cops were nowhere to be seen and he'd grabbed the loot successfully. That is until he ran outside ... where he was promptly run over by his getaway car.

Just to seal his fate, the man then accidentally shot himself.

You almost feel sorry him. Almost.

UP THE CREEK WITHOUT A PADDLE

A 37-year-old burglar on Teesside escaped in a canoe after being disturbed when he tried to break into a riverside home.

The police chase ended when a scouting helicopter discovered him hiding under a car, having dumped the getaway canoe.

The man was arrested by the Rapids Response Unit.

ANOTHER THICK IN THE WALL

Marathon runners are well aware of the phenomenon of 'hitting the wall', when it feels as if they can go no further. It's not a phenomenon that tends to affect villains. That is, unless, they are particularly stupid ...

A bag snatcher was caught after accidentally knocking himself out by running into a wall. The 27-year-old suspect was charged with robbery once he woke up in Gloucester Hospital.

Yes! Got the bag! What could possibly go ... smack!

FUNFACT:

It is a criminal offence to drive around in a dirty car in Russia.

BEG, BARROW AND STEAL

And in more slow-moving news ...

A 23-year-old burglar was sentenced to two years community service after using a wheelbarrow as a getaway vehicle.

Farmer Chris Lees returned to his farmhouse to find it had been ransacked. Angry and looking for those responsible, Chris left the house in a rage. Astonishingly, Mr Lees found the thief three miles up the road pushing the wheelbarrow stacked with all his belongings. The thief denied he'd nicked them and then, cheekily, asked for a lift.

Mr Lees agreed he was 'pushing it' and called the police.

OH (JOHN) DEERE ...

When a thief steals a vehicle for a joyride, you'd probably expect them to go for something with a bit of 'oomph' – a Ferrari, perhaps, or an MG.

Not in Devon, however, where this joyrider was about as slow as the vehicle he decided to steal ... a tractor.

In possibly the slowest police chase ever, the 18-year-old tractor thief was followed by a helicopter and *six* police cars ... at a whopping 12mph for over an hour as the snail's pace chase left the police bemused, yet distinctly unamused, as they found it difficult to stop him.

Thankfully the joyrider wasn't driving a magic tractor ... you know, the type that turns into a field.

A SINGLE TO PRISON PLEASE

After a failed bank-robbing attempt in Whitby, North Yorkshire, Simon North legged it and hopped on the first bus he could find.

North was carrying a fake gun but failed to get any cash at the bank. Having bungled the heist, he hopped on the bus to escape the pursuing police. It wasn't the hardest chase the police have ever had to do though: they simply followed the bus until he got off in Scarborough.

North was sentenced to three years. Just the ticket if you ask me.

SORRY, ME AGAIN...

A GUIDE TO ROBBING

Rule Number (1): If you've just robbed a petrol station, don't head back there ten minutes later and ask for directions.

An armed robber in the US – who had led police on a high-speed chase – did himself no favours when he unwittingly returned to the scene of the crime and asked for directions.

Ten minutes after holding up the gas station in Washington state, the bandit fled the scene, managing to lose the hot fuzz in pursuit, but when he became lost a few moments later, he pulled into the forecourt of the same petrol station he'd just robbed and asked for directions.

It's enough to drive you round the bend, isn't it?

THE HOUSE ALWAYS WINS

Do you ever get the feeling that some days it might be better just to stay in bed?

Take the gang in Nottingham whose attempted casino raid couldn't really have gone any worse. First, one of the gang member's masks fell off during the heist. Then they found that that their escape route was locked. When they did eventually manage to get out, their attempt to set fire to their getaway car resulted with them getting severe burns and having to call for an ambulance.

When it comes to a successful casino raid, I wouldn't bet on these guys.

LAWFUL IMPEDIMENT

The following villain has a thing about nicking wedding dresses ... but, stupidly, he forgot the golden rule about stealing from bridal shops:

When driving away from the scene of the crime, don't put a fully dressed mannequin in the passenger seat.

The man had made off with twenty dresses worth almost £20,000. Fifteen minutes after his getaway, police in Exeter spotted his unusual night-time passenger and swooped in for the arrest.

Maybe he just wanted to marry a model?

MIRROR, SIGNAL, UNABLE TO MANOEUVRE

I'm not sure our next villain had thought long and hard about his getaway, probably because he's stupid, but mainly because he can't drive.

After ransacking a house in Abbotsbury, Dorset, a thief tried to make a sharp exit. The 23-year-old was trying to escape in a Mercedes but not getting very far. He couldn't work out reverse and woke neighbours as he stalled and scraped the wing mirrors.

He deserves an 'A' for trying, but an 'L' plate for driving.

BAGGY TROUSERS ... OH, WHAT FUN WE HAD ...

A man who has been stealing DVDs from his local video store was tripped up recently ... by his own baggy trousers. They fell down twice, amusing the police officers who were hot on his tail.

The DVD pirate initially made his getaway on a bicycle but when officers spotted him in an alleyway, he abandoned the bike and ran. But it wasn't long before his trousers got the better of him, tripping him to the floor.

Obviously desperate to evade the police, he kicked off his trousers and shoes before jumping a fence into a backyard of a house where he was captured – quite literally – with his pants down.

A VILLAIN'S ROLL

A disabled man in New Zealand was foiled in his attempts to make a speedy getaway from the scene of the crime. Supermarket staff ran after him for more than half a mile when he was spotted with his wheelchair loaded with groceries.

The man was only stopped when he was cornered.

HA, HA, YOU'RE IT

A group of school pupils are being praised for foiling a gang of armed robbers. The children from a Liverpool primary school memorised the registration number of the thieves' getaway car by turning it into a playground chant.

The children repeated the chant while another pupil ran into the school to get a pen and paper and take down the details. Police traced the thieves less than 40 minutes after the robbery.

As a *Scooby Doo* villain might say: *'If it wasn't for those pesky kids ...'*

SNOW JOKE

German police captured two men suspected of stealing possessions from 15 cars by following their footprints in the snow for several miles.

Officers investigating a car in Hontrop found a smashed window and two sets of footprints. They followed the prints to the entrance of a flat where the burglars not only stored their booty, but also left their shoes and gloves to dry.

Boot-iful.

MORE FLAKY VILLAINS

These weren't the only thick villains to be caught out by a fall of snow ....

18-year-old William Devall went to court after admitting to criminal damage in Hailsham, East Sussex. After smashing a shop window during a snow flurry, police reported that they just followed Devall's prints all the way home and arrested him on his doorstep.

Ice work, officers.

THE FINGER POINTS AT ...

Those of you reading this while eating might want to skip onto the next story ...

A burglar tore off his finger when his ring snagged while he was trying to escape from a museum when the alarm sounded. Breaking the golden rule of 'never go back', he was caught when he returned to retrieve it.

To make matters worse, doctors could not re-attach the digit.

BRINGING HOME THE BACON. ALMOST.

A former Russian soldier is our next thick villain.

Igor Vaclavic carried out a spate of robberies in Italy recently ... dressed as a ninja. No, I'm not sure why either.

Igor, riding a getaway bicycle, met his match when he decided to burgle the farmhouse of Giovanni Zampier – a 73-year-old.

Giovanni chased him – and this I would loved to have seen – on his tractor before, eventually, Igor's bike tracks led to a hideout where police found a stash of salami and cured ham – which is appropriate considering the pig's ear Igor made of his robbery.

PRIZE IDIOT

Planning to mug joggers is a risky, and stupid, idea. But that's what one particular thick villain decided to do.

Experienced marathon runner Glyn Roberts was mugged of his bag in Hampstead Heath and, well, its pretty obvious what happened.

He chased the mugger for two miles.

'We ran and ran. He kept turning round with this stunned look on his face! Eventually, he fell to his knees and begged me to let him go but that wasn't going to happen,' Glyn explained to the police.

The mugger will now have plenty of time to practise his running in the exercise yard.

IT SEEMED LIKE A GOOD IDEA AT THE TIME

These days muggers are armed with an array of weapons and the police always advise us to never 'fight back'. But there are occasions when sometimes it pays off.

Thick villains ... have a taste of your own medicine!

HOME-RUN HEROES

I'm not sure Jesus would approve of the following, but it's proof that sometimes God does work in mysterious ways ...

A burglar – an atheist I presume – targeted a church in Florida last year but was ambushed by parishioners armed with baseball bats.

Like a big girl's blouse, Ralph Thomas fled the scene and locked himself in a room. He was treated for broken ribs and bruising after receiving a battering.

A spokesman for Palm Beach police said, 'They got the best of him alright.'

I reckon those parishioners gave him hell.

IT'S A KNOCKOUT!

I would have loved to have seen the look on this young mugger's face when he realised he'd started picking on 88-year-old Gerhard Brinkmann of Halberstadt, Germany – the country's top lightweight boxer in the 1930s.

Gerhard knocked the thick toerag out stone-cold.

The OAP told officers: `I told him to come closer if he wanted it and, as he did, I landed a full-force right hook on his chin.'

OAP.

KO.

PINT-SIZED HEROINE

The following thick villain probably fancied his chances when he broke into 58-year-old Mo Richards' pub in Southampton, England. What he couldn't have guessed was that the diminutive landlady was also an expert in the martial art of Aikido.

Landlady Mo, just 5ft 4in, held the thug in a headlock for ten minutes until the police arrived. He attempted to wriggle free but she just tightened her grip.

A man later appeared in court. I'll doubt he'll be able to wriggle out of this one.

AMERICAN BEAUTIES TURN UGLY

Getting beaten up by a bunch of pensioners has got to be the ultimate humiliation. But getting beat up by a bunch of beauty-school babes has got to be just as embarrassing.

An armed robber in Little Rock, Arkansas was subjected to the cringe-worthy criminal balls-up after telling a class of young ladies to 'stick 'em up' during their beauty lesson. Little did he know what was to happen next – the girls 'stuck' it to him instead and gave him a beating of a lifetime. Teacher Dianne Mitchell began the ordeal when she tripped him up as he attempted to clean out their handbags. Several other girls then piled in and started beating the assailant with curling tongs!

A police spokesman reported that the thief tried to make a getaway but the girls kept pulling him back for more – proof that beauty is in the (black) eye of the beholder.

POLICE ACADEMY

An armed robber in Japan chose the wrong place to hold-up as he blundered his way into a police dormitory. 26-year-old Yoshimasa Yamada broke into the Swords and Firearms department of the local Japanese law-enforcement offices. He screamed out 'Show me the money!' (in Japanese, obviously) before being instantly surrounded by cops who were armed to the teeth.

'私にお金を示しなさい!'

WHAT'S FOR LUNCH?

Speaking of teeth, this following mistake is the sort of judgement in error you only really want to make once. Not that I have much sympathy for this knife-wielding mugger in Bloemfontein, South Africa. He came to a sticky end after deciding to hide in a zoo ... in the tiger enclosure.

He had just mugged a couple and leapt into the tiger enclosure to escape.

And what do tigers think of thieves for lunch?

'They're GREAT!'

YOU'RE NICKED, MUSH

Our next villain felt decidedly out of plaice, sorry place, when he floundered at a fish and chip shop owned by George and Helen Tung in Bolton.

The thief lashed out at George with his hammer when the burglary commenced but luckily Helen intervened ... by throwing a pan of mushy peas at him! Thankfully this rendered the robber so confused that Helen was able to finish him off by scalding him with hot water used to cook the steak and kidney pies.

Our thief knew it was time to cut and run and fled the scene only for the police to catch up with him later that evening with some tell-tale burns.

Instead of being squids in, the villain was jailed for three years.

He must be gutted.

ASSAULT WITH BATTERY

Another chip-shop battering, this time in York ...

A chip-shop worker has revealed how he faced down an armed robber – with a fish slice dripping in hot fat. 63-year-old Malcolm Butters was closing up at the Green Lane Fish Bar when he was confronted by a man brandishing a gun.

'Give us the money, mate,' the thug demanded. 'But instead,' Malcolm explained to the police, 'I got my fish slice, dipped it in the hot fat and waved it at him, hoping the fat would come off and splash him.'

The greasy villain made off without as much as a fish supper.

ICEBERG, DEAD AHEAD

82-year-old George Smith from Speldhurst, Kent was forced to improvise with the iceberg lettuce he'd just bought when he foiled a post-office robbery by clobbering the armed raider with the reliable sandwich filler.

George, a war veteran, instinctively knew his lettuce was a good weapon of choice – hitting the robber twice in the face before the thief managed to escape on his bike.

'The best method of defence is attack,' George remarked after the incident.

For the thick villain's sake, lettuce pray that George never sees him again.

SUGAR WITH THAT, DEAR?

In New York state, some thick villains picked the wrong elderly couple to pick on.

81-year-old retired farmer Raymond Papin and his wife Joyce, 74, fought back when they found masked men in camouflage gear turning their home upside down. Raymond responded to the intruders' demand for money in an uncompromising fashion – he whacked one of the men with a sugar bowl.

Meanwhile, Joyce seized a shotgun and told them to leave – which they did.

What a sweet little story.

PRIZE IDIOT

ALL BLACK AND BLUE

So now we know, pensioners can be perilous when they need to be ...

And burglar Clinton Dearman knows that only too well.

Members of a bowls club in Christchurch, New Zealand arrived to find a trophy cabinet smashed and looted before discovering the criminal Clinton hiding in the ladies loo.

The grey army of pensioners duffed him up and tied him up and waited for the police to arrive. Dearman was remanded in custody but at the trial the goon pleaded for his sentence to be reduced – arguing that he'd already suffered enough public humiliation in jail!

Robbing a bowls club: two years and four months in jail.

Getting beaten up by pensioners: priceless.

STUPID BOY

Schoolboy error alert! Warning! Read with caution ...

Attention to detail is everything if you're a wannabe criminal genius, and there is no room for schoolboy errors ...

Though, clearly, somebody forgot to tell the following set of thick villains...

ARRESTED, DUDE

In one way, this next young villain was showing great initiative; in another way he was being an absolute fool. You decide ...

A teenager in Gulfport, Florida believed that the best way to sell his drug stash was to dial numbers randomly on his phone. You could say its 'cold calling' gone cold turkey.

Sure enough, he eventually phoned a policeman at home who arranged a rendezvous the same day. Detective Matt Parks met the 14-year-old boy at the boy's school and once it became clear it was a real deal (being shown the marijuana and crack cocaine will do the trick), duly arrested the very surprised juvenile.

The youth was charged with possession and intent to distribute drugs near a school.

I reckon the only lines this boy will be doing after school for a while will be:

I promise not to sell drugs near school.

I promise not to sell drugs near school.

I promise not to sell drugs near school.

I promise not to sell drugs near school.

MUMMY'S BOY

Another story now, in which 'mum' really is the word ... the final one.

20-year-old Michal Zahradnikova had a bit of a shock while watching the Czech edition of *Crimewatch* with his mum. The programme aired CCTV footage of Michal clearly robbing a McDonald's restaurant. Michal's mother grabbed him by the ear and immediately marched him to the police station.

A police spokesman reported: 'Michal admitted he was responsible for robbing a number of fast-food stores and put up no resistance to the charges. Michal also claims to have been using the stolen money to buy a Mother's Day present.'

Yeah, right.

BED HEAD

After any crime there is always an element of blind panic about what to do next, but why is it that our stupid villains often foul up *after* they've escaped?

A prisoner of Stamford Hill jail was cunning enough to escape the maximum-security prison but was stupid enough to be caught six hours later hiding under a bed at his mum's house.

Imagine *Escape from Alcatraz*.

And then imagine the polar opposite.

FIRST PLACE YOU'D LOOK?

This young man went to even greater lengths to escape – and he would have gotten away with it – if only he wasn't so arrogant.

19-year-old robber Timothy Rouse walked free from jail in Kentucky, USA after his friends sent a bogus pardon, via fax, from a local grocery store. The fax contained no letterhead, no government stamp and dozens of spelling mistakes.

It took the authorities two weeks to realise their 'administrative error' and police found him almost straight away at his mum's house.

Red-faced officials at the prison say they often receive genuine court documents which are 'full of errors'.

Well, that's comforting to know.

KEEPING IT IN THE FAMILY

Using the family home as a hideout is as obvious as it is stupid, but getting mum involved as the getaway driver is just hilarious, I mean, unforgivable.

The mother, Daniela Langer, admitted to helping her teenage son carry out a jewellery-shop heist of about £25,000 ... just to make sure he didn't get hurt.

Langer told the court: 'He was determined to do it, and I could not talk him out of it, so I offered to drive him there to keep an eye on him. I was worried about him getting caught.'

I blame the parents.

I WOULDN'T SAY HER COOKING WAS BAD ...

Imagine a mother's shame of finding out that her own son has broken back *into* jail because he preferred it than living with her. Ouch, that's got to hurt.

That's what dappy 23-year-old Detlef Federsohn from Austria did though. He missed his 6ft x 6ft cell in prison so much that after his initial release he attempted a reverse jailbreak - and was arrested when he was spotted on the prison roof.

Federsohn said upon his re-capture: 'Life is so much easier on the inside. They feed you, do your washing and let you watch TV - which I can tell you is a lot more than my mum does.'

As far as I'm concerned anyone who wants to break into prison deserves to be there for as long as they like.

PREMATURE JUBILATION

Acting like a jerk in the courtroom won't do you any favours, as Craig Conn will tell you.

The 21-year-old was convicted of assault in Airdrie, Scotland but the judge decided to let him out on bail ahead of the sentencing hearing.

When Craig was told the news he 'whooped' for joy.

Sheriff Robert Dickson immediately ordered him back into the dock and told him that, actually, he would now be remanded into the custody of a prison for four weeks.

Woo-hoo!

CAN'T GET ENOUGH

Ok, ok, the last few stories have been utterly ridiculous in terms of sheer villainous stupidity but this one takes the biscuit.

While on day release, two impatient prisoners were jailed at Kingston Crown Court for pulling a job. Delroy Peters and Matthew Windrass were convicted of attempting to steal watches from a jeweller in Richmond-upon-Thames – a crime they had planned to commit while in prison.

The police were informed prior to the robbery though, via a tip-off, and were waiting for them.

They tried to steal time, and that's exactly what they got.

NORWEGIAN HOODS

Two young vandals overlooked a small but crucial detail when they started smashing up an elevator at a railway station in Norway – they were inside it.

The lift at Lillestroem Train Station got a right beating but, in the end, it had the last laugh. As a defence mechanism against vandalism, the lift sealed its doors, trapping the young delinquents inside.

'Vandalism is always sad, but a lot of people do see the humour in this particular incident,' said Ellen Svendsvoll, a spokesperson for Norway's National Rail Administration.

'They got what was coming to them,' said the lift.

SMILE!

From scandals and vandals in Norway to joyriders in the UK.

A group of Bournemouth boys ended up with their moronic faces all over the local papers when they actually posed for a speed camera. Unbelievably, the three teenagers, who'd just nicked a Ford Escort, turned around as they sped past the camera and were clearly identifiable.

The police subsequently escorted them to court.

YOU'VE BEEN GATSOED

A motorist in Switzerland has set a new world record – and been awarded an instant driving ban – after receiving four speeding tickets in just one minute and thirty seven seconds.

Apparently, the driver was confused by the first flash and returned three times, at speed, to check what was going on. Seems unlikely, you'd think?

A Swiss-police spokesperson said the feat required not only 'precision driving' but also 'utter stupidity'.

I concur.

WHO'S LAUGHING NOW?

Don't we all love practical jokers? Well, Mr Miller doesn't ...

An office prank went horrifically wrong when both the prankster and the victim wound up in court. Joker James Koons created a fake half-million-pound winning lottery ticket, then left it lying around his workplace in Pennsylvania, USA. It was found by an ecstatic Brian Miller who tried to claim the money.

After claiming his innocence, Miller was cleared of making a false claim but Koons was fined and sentenced to a year of probation for forgery.

We've all learnt a valuable lesson here ... practical jokers are idiots.

PLAYING WITH FIRE

Thick villains shouldn't play with fire; they will get hurt.

In New Zealand, three men trying to steal fuel from a farm ended up setting fire to their own car. The bungling trio had siphoned diesel into a petrol-only vehicle.

When the car refused to start, the men examined the fuel pipe using a cigarette lighter. I'll give you three guesses as to what happens next ... but you should only need one.

BOOM – the car burst into flames.

The young men were not-so-much red-faced as second-degree-burn-faced and, to add to their embarrassment, were charged with theft.

PLAYING WITH FIRE PART TWO

I wonder if Shane Long's mother ever told him not to play with fire?

A court in Brisbane heard how Long, a wannabe arsonist, was hired to torch a hair salon but failed not once, not twice, but three times.

On the third occasion Shane set himself alight, which rather helped the police with their inquiries with their burning questions.

MARATHON MAN

News of a shameless benefits cheat getting nabbed here; and we should all take it personally ...

A 47-year-old man from Mansfield was jailed for ten months for claiming he was crippled and raking in more than £20,000 in benefits – that's £20,000 of taxpayers' money - when all the time he was a keen runner.

The man claimed on benefit-application forms that he was unable to walk without the use of two walking sticks or a frame, and was largely confined to a wheelchair.

Though in reality, our intrepid villain was such a keen amateur runner, he was only caught when photographed running the 2005 London Marathon. Passing sentence, Judge David Price showed remarkable restraint, saying,:`You were clearly fit enough to work.'

If us taxpayers should ever met him down a dark alleyway, he better run fast!

ANTIQUES ROGUE SHOW

An armed robber who got away from a post office with £800 discovered his shotgun was worth rather more.

The vintage weapon he was brandishing around willy-nilly was worth £10,000. Though that is before the robber sawed off half the barrel.

Here today, gun tomorrow.

I'M HAVING A SHOT

Police in Vancouver reminded people (as if it's something we forget) that it's not a good idea to play with a loaded gun while using the toilet, after a man accidentally shot himself.

A 21-year-old shot off one of his fingers while 'playing' with 'a gun' while on the 'throne'. A Mountie's police statement explaining the incident read:

'Perhaps our mothers never explained to us that it was not a good idea to play with handguns whilst using the restroom. But then again, maybe that was supposed to be a given.'

I GIVE UP

This next villain is thick ... but only because he's so honest.

A car thief who drove a stolen vehicle straight to a police station to confess was told he's probably too stupid to go to jail. Mohammed Zaman's unexpected U-turn stunned officers who did not even know the roadside heist had even occurred.

As the conscience-stricken 22-year-old was arrested, he explained, 'Someone put me up to it.'

Adjourning the case, the judge told Zaman: 'Frankly, you are an idiot and I hope you realise that.'

All in favour say 'Aye'.

Case closed.

MASKING THE OBVIOUS

Masks work as great disguises... but only if you wear them for the whole robbery. They become nothing but ladies stockings if you take them off.

In Manchester, a 24-year-old Gavin Rae remembered to put his mask on before using a fake gun to hold up a bookmaker.

However, the imbecile took off the mask before he was out of the shop. CCTV clearly identified his face as he took off the stocking.

That little slip-up, or should I say slip-off, cost Rae 10 years in prison.

 **FUNFACT:**
Al Capone's business card said he was a used-furniture dealer.

BALKAN BERK

After robbing 35 bookies in and around the city of Zagreb, Croatia – without disguising his face – a moronic crook pushed his luck too far by returning to one bookies to place a bet.

A police spokesperson commented: 'It was unbelievable. He robbed 35 different bookmakers and then happily walked back into one ready to spend the exact same money he'd got from robbing them.'

In return, the police threw the book at him.

BROTHEL CREEP

Returning to the scene of the crime is an amateur's mistake and this next thick villain takes some beating.

A man, convicted of robbing a brothel in Tottenham, went back to the same brothel for a bit of hanky-panky. In fact, this thief robbed the knocking shop twice – once without a mask.

The man must have liked what he saw because, unbelievably, he then returned for the company of one of the establishment's ladyfolk.

He didn't get what he was after but he did get to visit the local police station where officers took great pleasure in sizing his particulars.

FRENCH NICKER

They say TV rots the brain. They could not be more right ...

After making off with a television, a French burglar (pronounced *bur-gu-laire*) was caught when he returned to the scene of the crime to steal the remote control.

While the householder was at the police station reporting the first burglary, neighbours spotted the dim-witted thief return.

A police spokesman reported, 'I guess there's daring and then there's stupid.'

My point exactly.

CAUGHT KRAUT

You've got to admire the front of these guys who return to the scene of their crimes. Is it an elaborate double-bluff or are they just really that stupid?

A thief in Bielefeld, Germany was caught when he returned a pair of trainers in two different sizes to the shop he had stolen them from, dressed in clothes he'd also nicked.

Police say the shoes and jacket were only available in that store and store workers cottoned immediately.

'It seems he may not have been the brightest of thieves,' said one copper.

BUM NOTE

To Holland for a thick, but musically gifted, villain.

Police were called to a house in Tiel after the owner heard a burglar playing on his piano downstairs.

The homeowner first heard the ivory-tinkling thief ransacking the living room before settling down to play a few classics unaware that he had an audience.

You have to Handel it to him, his idiocy does deserves a standing ovation.

Bravo!

DABS DOB COP

Now, you would have thought, wouldn't you, that no-one had so much front that they would actually apply for police college in the certain knowledge they were already on the offenders list.

Think again as we head back to New Zealand where police employment fell by 1% after a new recruit got more than expected when he was betrayed by his own fingerprint. Taking part in a standard fingerprinting exercise during a class, the wannabe-cop print matched him to an outstanding warrant for his arrest – for serious assault.

His career prospects were looking decidedly grim at this point.

IS THAT A WODGE OF MONEY IN YOUR POCKET OR ARE YOU JUST PLEASED TO SEE ME?

Exploding money packets containing dyes are now routinely used to ensure big cash robberies are pointless as it's almost impossible to use when they're a different colour.

Mind you, a thick villain doesn't know that, does he?

A bank robber in Orlando collapsed in agony after a money packet exploded in his pants. Kenneth Brooks had stuffed the package in his underwear before doing a runner but it somehow caught light.

The robber was treated for burns to his bottom and, how should I put this, 'delicate' parts – which had turned a rather embarrassing shade of red. And black. And blue. And purple. And yellow.

He was singing more than a rainbow, you can bet. Ouch.

DOLLY GETS NO LOLLY

Thick villains use all sorts of things in hold-ups but I've not heard of a baby's doll before ...

A 25-year-old bank robber in Karachi, Pakistan demanded £20,000 claiming the doll he was holding was a bomb and the blood-pressure gauge he had in his other hand was a grenade.

Quite rightly, no-one believed him and he was nicked.

FRUIT LOOPY

24-year-old Robert Downey (not that one, readers) was jailed for seven years for endeavouring to hold up a bookies in London's East End with a banana – a thief's favourite fruit.

He had it wrapped in a plastic bag but all the staff could see what it was and simply called the police. It's not the first time 'banana man' has used this tactic and failed: he was jailed five years earlier for a similar fruity heist.

Downey was arrested within minutes of fleeing, and he was caught still struggling to take off his balaclava because it was too small.

It's stories like this that make you feel good to be alive.

LET ME JUST WRITE THAT DOWN FOR YOU

I'm always amazed by the regular stories of guys who are practically throwing themselves into jail. For example, when did robbers begin thinking that actually handing bank staff personal information would be a good idea? Did we miss that meeting?

In Philadelphia, a bungling bank robber handed a bank teller his pay slip – which had on his name and address crossed out – and also written instructions that demanded he be given all the cash from the tills.

Police claimed that finding the robber was not a huge forensic undertaking.

'We just put the pay slip under a light' they said.

A man caught with $1,800 dollars on him then helped police with their enquiries.

DOH!

In Uckfield, 28-year-old Zac James pleaded guilty to burglary.

Zac didn't have much choice really; he'd left an envelope containing his address and phone number at the scene of the crime.

Wow, he really phoned that robbery in, didn't he?

SLIPPER OF THE YARD

Slippers and a trampoline will spice up any pursuit but it's the documentary evidence which sent down crook Gary Windsor.

Off-duty cop Nick Wattam discovered the 25-year-old felon ransacking his garage in Harrogate and duly gave chase in his slippers. The burglar was obviously adept at fleeing and used the kids' trampoline at the end of the garden to successfully vault the fence. In doing so, he also dropped his bag containing his wallet which had his name and address not even convincingly concealed.

Windsor was jailed for nine months when police knocked on his door moments after the theft.

Mr Wattam, in his police statement, revealed, 'If I hadn't been wearing my slippers, he'd never have even got to the trampoline.'

FINGER NICKIN' GOOD

OK boys, so don't write down stuff at the scene, don't take a letter addressed to you ... what else? Oh yes, don't take all major forms of ID with you as well.

Police found it very easy to track down the man who assaulted two KFC workers in Cincinatti before stealing money from the safe. As 42-year-old Nathan McFarland fled the scene, he dropped his wallet, which contained a photo ID card, his social-security card and birth certificate.

Gotcha.

YOURS SINCERELY ...

Thick villains often forget things which are written down only to be used in evidence against them later on ...

A prisoner in Madison, Wisconsin, had his appeal turned down after sending a death threat to a judge. Anthony Dwane Turner denied sending the letter to the judge who had jailed him for 15 years for assault and battery charges.

His defence lawyer claimed nobody had seen him write the letter, but the jury were swayed by the fact the envelope the threat was sent in was marked with Anthony Dwane Turner's name, inmate number and the address of the prison in Green Bay.

No need to pack quite yet, Anthony.

I'M GUESSING HE WAS DRUNK ...

When Eric Cunningham robbed a filling station in Orlando, Florida he walked away $80 richer and with two packets of cigarettes. Not a great haul, is it?

What he left behind though was more than enough to help police track down the 18-year-old. Propped up against the counter, he left his gun case, with the receipt for the AK47 with which he carried out the robbery, complete with his name and address.

I wish I was making this stuff up, I really do.

FAKE FIREARM, REAL ADDRESS

Another teenager in trouble was our next villain from South Glamorgan.

Maybe he just got carried away with the excitement of it all or maybe he is just plain thick. Again, you decide.

The 19-year-old robber was caught when he left his jacket with his name and address in the pocket near the scene of his crime. He'd used a fake gun to hold up a filling station and when police traced his escape route they found his jacket.

Discarding the jacket may have helped him run quicker but it also ensured he was jailed for six years.

NEVER LOOK BACK ... OR EVEN GO BACK

An armed robber who left his driving licence at the scene of the crime in Michigan returned to plead his innocence.

To make matters worse – he was chased away from the filling station he was robbing by a woman who was *seven months pregnant*.

The man was arrested upon his return.

BAGS OF TROUBLE

A robber in Norwich terrified a newsagent but was left floundering after he left behind his prison laundry bag with his name on it after fleeing the crime scene.

28-year-old Owen Moore had also written a note demanding cash on prison notepaper which he thoughtfully left in the bag. It didn't take long for the police to track him down and Moore was sent back to jail for another four and a half years.

I'm sure they let him use his old bag.

EXPLOSIVE FICTION

This thick villain didn't exactly do much to cover his tracks ... but then what thick villain does?

A man who held up banks in Massachusetts and New Hampshire claiming he had a bomb in his bag was arrested. Police found the bag actually contained books, some labelled with George Melendez's full name and address.

And they say you can't judge a book by its cover ...

FUNFACT:

In ancient Egypt, killing a cat was a crime punishable by death.

LET ME JUST ...

In Minnesota, a would-be bank robber was apprehended after a major goof.

Thomas Mason handed a note demanding cash to a member of staff. The note threatened to kill everyone which was not very nice. Thankfully what Mason forgot was the note had his name on it.

Police arrested him a short time later and no doubt issued their own threats.

HIGH ON LIFE

The following chump was a little too keen to get out ...

A dopey drugs dealer in Knoxville, Tennessee was about to be released when he stupidly wrote to his partner-in-crime asking him to contact old clients and sort out an immediate supply.

Of course, prison authorities routinely censor the mail. What's gratifying the most about this story – apart from the dealer's immense stupidity – was that the dealer was about to be released from a six-month term but instead went on to serve another eight years.

His name: Aaron Lawless.

PRIZE IDIOT

HAVE YOU GOT A PEN?

In a very crowded category, Alejandro Martinez stands out for sheer, jaw-dropping stupidity.

The 23-year-old had just completed a job-application form at a pizzeria in Las Vegas when he had a brainstorm. Alejandro decided that now, yes now, right that minute, was the time to rob the joint.

The hapless schmuck got away with $110 but it didn't take police long to track him down – Martinez had put his real name and address on the application form.

TECHNOPHOBES

Forget *Dragnet*, the Internet is the new way to catch thieves, wrong doers and criminals. Wi-fi, GPS and mobile phone technology also now means that potential victims can, and do, keep a remote eye in the sky.

Just remember, thick villains, Big Brother is watching you. And, no doubt, finding your incessant stupidity painful to watch ...

CELL PHONE

I'm absolutely convinced the Internet, satellite-navigation systems and mobile phones are making the stupid people even more stupid ...

In Milan, police arrested a bag-snatcher after he called them to arrange a date. The clumsy clown then dropped his phone when he mugged an old lady and then called it in a bid to meet up with the finder.

By the time the officers met him at the agreed point, he'd robbed another old lady and was riding a stolen scooter.

Cocky scumbag.

OH, THAT'S A NICE PICTURE

Who would ever have thought that one day in the near-future mobile phones would be able to take photos and videos? Well, the future's here and the police love it.

Our next burglar was known to detectives in Slough, but unfortunately they had never been able to finger him directly. So when the man left his mobile telephone after a 'job' the police knew it was a gift from the gods.

Among the photos on his mobile device was a very clear one of him gooning at the camera. The police swooped in and arrested him immediately.

The dimbo was sentenced to 160 hours of community service, but to be honest, I would not want him snooping around my bins.

AND ANOTHER ONE ...

David Kelly from Dorset was sentenced to six years' jail time after his mobile phone – which had his picture on it – was left at the scene of the crime.

Kelly dropped the supposedly handheld device as he switched getaway cars after the robbery.

Oh, and he used his own car too.

FARE COP

Detectives are increasingly using the data trails left by mobile phones to build cases and demolish alibis though this is a rarely a straightforward process.

Swedish police caught a burglar after he mistakenly answered a phone he had just stolen letting the coppers eavesdrop on his getaway ride in a taxi.

First, never book a taxi to use as a getaway vehicle (especially in London, where you'll end up poorer than when you got in) and, second, organise your heists a bit better. When police first phoned the burglar all they heard was him swearing at the cabbie for being late.

The taxi was tracked down and the man was arrested.

TINKER, TAILOR, SOLDIER, THICK VILLAIN

This guy had to be drunk ...

Breaking into a shop full of high-tech gadgetry in London was never going to win you a Nobel Prize.

Surrounded by cameras, tracking devices and the like he plumped for a games console which, as they all do nowadays, had a GPS tag. The in-store detectives simply turned on the satellite locator and told the police.

The shoplifter was soon arrested and never saw the games console again.

CALENDAR BOY

Occasionally you hear a story which makes you go 'ahhh'.

Our next burglar stuck to what he knew and ignored all the expensive computers in the office he was nicking from. The Teignmouth-based thief had broken into a building firm but the only thing he walked out with was a Kelly Brook calendar.

Nice taste, but shame about the brains.

DOT CONS

Some young thick villains who were too handy on computers for their own good got what was coming to them. Namely a stint in prison.

A gang of ASBO yobs in North Wales were convicted after setting up a website to boast about their crimes – including drugs, burglary, vandalism and arson.

The seven-strong 'collective' even put photos and video on the website and soon attracted a download from the local police station.

You could call it a plod-cast.

WE KNOW WHAT YOU'RE DOING

Some of the most innovative crime-busting is now on home computers. Link up a few cameras to your PC and get it to email or dial your mobile when they start seeing something out of the ordinary.

A 28-year-old London burglar picked the wrong victim when he took laptops from the flat of a computer-science graduate. Richard East was convinced Payne would return to collect some vital cables so he set a high-tech trap.

The hidden webcam got some great shots. A detective said: 'We didn't have a job to do really. He was at his mum's when we picked him up and clearly had no idea he'd been filmed.'

Man vs machine?

One nil to them.

WE KNOW TOO

Two men were convicted in Lancaster for burgling a house while its suprised owner watched the raid on his laptop 1600 miles away.

The men were arrested when John Ellison called the police from Malaga, Spain. He'd installed a £20,000 pound CCTV system which alerted his mobile phone if the alarm was triggered.

Isn't technology marvellous?

WE KNOW: PART THREE

Brazilian businessman Joao Pedro Wettlauser was in Germany when he got a text alert about a break-in at his home; he logged on, watched the burglar and phoned the police.

The villain was caught in the house and was actually trying on the owner's suits when the police burst in.

The handcuffs suited him, I reckon.

CAUGHT ON CAMERA

The more astute burglar will first check for cameras and either spray over them or cut the cables.

Then there's our next thick villain who tried in vain to nick a CCTV camera while, all the time, it was filming lovely close-ups of his anguished face.

A Plymouth court heard the man plead guilty to two charges of stealing surveillance cameras though, based on the evidence submitted, he didn't have much choice.

PRIZE IDIOT

NOT SAVED BY THE BELL

This is so beautifully simple, this thick villain simply has to win the crown of 'King Technophobe'.

You know those people who are so addicted to their mobile phones they never, ever switch them off?

Police in Massachusetts do. They found it quite easy to find Eric Nolan when he ran off into woods after having broken a court order. Officers simply rang his mobile and listened out for the ringtone.

Sure enough, Eric couldn't turn it off quickly enough.

THE SMARTER SEX?

The vast majority of criminals are men but there are a few 'villainesses' around and so, clearly, a few of them will be thick as, well, thieves.

It's not a long chapter and some of the 'villains' aren't really criminals but this section is one for the gents – just to prove that men don't have the complete monopoly on being really, really, stunningly stupid.

TISSUE OF LIES

There aren't many thick villainesses but they sure do make up for it in quality ...

An American woman called Suzanne Butts was told she faced two years in jail for stealing toilet paper from a courthouse. Police in Iowa claimed Butts was caught red-handed stealing three rolls of loo paper from the Marshall County Courthouse.

Because of prior convictions, Butts was told to expect prison. Supervisor Gordie Johnson said: 'We have three strikes and you're out. I consider each roll of toilet paper a strike.'

A woman called Butts caught stealing toilet paper ... what more could you want?

THE CUSTOMER IS ALWAYS RIGHT

Eloise Reaves certainly takes her rights as a consumer seriously. She was arrested by cops in North Carolina after complaining to them about the quality of goods she'd bought.

But this wasn't a CD player or a jumper; Reaves complained a drugs dealer had sold her 'bad crack'.

The policeman warned her she would be arrested if the rock tested positive for cocaine. It did and she was.

FUNFACT:

The electric chair was invented by a dentist.

LIVER BIRD DOES BIRD

Over to Liverpool where a cleaner at the Crown Court was locked up in the same cells she used to mop ... for benefit fraud.

The 58-year-old had been claiming benefit cheques under her maiden name and was convicted of swindling more than £20,000 out of taxpayers. The fraudulent female used to turn up at social security in a wheelchair but she was later found out to be holding down three cleaning jobs.

What a mop-pet!

DON'T THEY KNOW WHO I AM?

Wouldn't it be grand to live in a world where you just park with impunity?

A world like Roma Wheldon's.

In just two years, Wheldon had racked up a whopping 120 parking tickets. Roma, from Southend-on-Sea, believed she was immune from paying the fines but had to call on her family to help her avoid jail.

Her final parking-tee fine topped £18,000.

Roma said, 'I never thought it would go this far.'

Well, if you don't pay your fines, neither will you.

AND THEY TOOK EVERYTHING

Another lady who thought she was immune from the long arm of the law was this thick villainess from Reading, but, as my mum once said, liars always get their comeuppance.

The 52-year-old was jailed for lying about a burglary. She claimed £30,000 worth of jewellery, mink coats and appliances were nicked but it was, of course, an insurance job.

There was no sign of forced entry but, more importantly, when arrested she was wearing a pendant she'd claimed was stolen.

However not so much nicked, as necked.

DOUBLE TROUBLE

The moral of this story is don't mess with a judge.

18-year-old Yamahile Ortiz got her twin sister to stand in for her because she couldn't be bothered to attend court. Ortiz had been using a stolen credit card in Connecticut and wanted her sister Yariizca to plead guilty and go for probation.

But Yamahile got a bit more than that when Judge Patrick Clifford rumbled them and jailed her for contempt.

PRIZE IDIOT

BE CAREFUL WHAT YOU WISH FOR

Well done to three members of the Women's Institute in Herstmonceux, East Sussex, who campaigned against reckless, speeding drivers through their village.

The good news is they now have their own speed camera.

The bad news is the ladies have all been snapped by it and been fined £60.

WE SALUTE YOU

Very occasionally you hear about a smart villain to whom you just have to doff your hat and say, 'Well done, sir.'

We get a kick from hearing about the cretinously stupid robbers but we can also enjoy the odd rascal who's able to stick two fingers up to authority.

These villains, unlike the rest of the idiots in this book, to my knowledge at least, are still at large....

TRENDY AND USELESS

Yes, it's not only villains who are thick. London stands alone among the world's major cities for the sheer amount of green space so what form of transportation would you not pick for your police officers?

London's parkie police binned their new roller-blades because they couldn't chase criminals across the grass. Officers who patrol the Royal Parks went back to traditional bicycles as the best way of getting around.

A senior officer said the in-line skates were hung up for good after the 'criminal community' realised their Achilles heel.

THROUGH THICK AND THIN

This guy was smart, thick and thin all in the space of a few days.

Robert Cole escaped from jail in Sydney by going on a crash diet and literally squeezing between the bars. After three days on the run, Cole was still thin but also very thick as he was spotted and arrested in a shopping centre.

Fair play, he did have a fake beard to disguise himself.

Mind you, it wasn't so realistic.

He had drawn it on with a felt-tip pen.

LOCK, STOCK AND TWO SMOKING EARS

A very cheeky villain, methinks ...

A council in Scotland issued a belated apology to one of its tenants after it changed the locks on his flat, at the request of a burglar.

James McLeod was away on holiday when Clackmannanshire council received the call from convicted burglar Richard Strachan, claiming he was locked out. A locksmith duly changed the locks, gave the only set of keys to Strachan, who walked in and helped himself to the hi-fi and microwave oven.

Once Mr McLeod returned and pointed out the rather glaring lock cock-up, Strachan was sentenced to 300 hours' community service.

COPPERWATCH

Sometimes it's the police making the headlines for being just as thick as the thieves ... which isn't very reassuring is it?

In Sydney, the boys in blue must have been queuing up for a bit of blue action.

Officers were paid to have sex with prostitutes because government officials wanted to gather, ahem, 'hard evidence' to close down unlicensed brothels. It was estimated $10,000 of taxpayers' cash was spent in a few years.

Following the reports of the scam in the press, Kuringai council defended their actions by admitting sometimes 'extreme measures' were necessary to catch law-breakers.

I'll say.

YOU'RE NICKED, SON

Sometimes even the police don't get it 100% accurate ...

Police in Derby sent a letter to Peter Akers calling on him to own up to his crimes and then they'd help him make a fresh start. Peter was six.

Peter's mum Christine says the boy has admitted to stealing sweets from his sister and she thought about taking him to the police station to confess about not tidying his room.

Derbyshire police apologised but believe letters to real criminals do sometimes work.

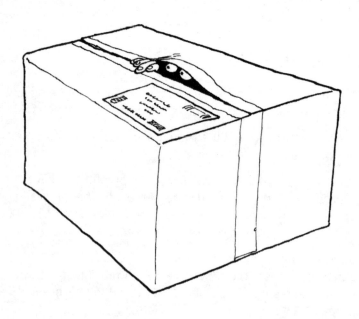

PRIZE VILLAINS

Hats off must go to Muradif Hasanbegovic and Max Friedener ...

These two crims are worthy of The *Great Escape*. Muradif wrapped himself in a large parcel and posted himself to freedom from a jail in Austria. He was serving a seven-year sentence for robbery. Muradif packed himself up in a parcel and other convicts loaded him onto a lorry.

Prison warden Franz Hochstrasser said: 'This sort of thing was not supposed to happen. Guards need to count prisoners at the end of working hours.'

Over the border to Germany and convicted fraudster Max escaped from a jail in Darmstadt after climbing into a cardboard box and posting himself to freedom.

The 28-year-old escaped by hiding in the box in the mailroom. He escaped from the mail van as it was driving away.

The escape was only noticed when the mail truck arrived at the sorting depot and the hole in the box was spotted.

That's what I call boxing clever.

For Simon's latest thick-villain stories,
listen to 'Heart Breakfast with
Jamie Theakston' on:

106.2FM in London
DAB Digital Radio
Freeview channel 728
Sky channel 0124
also online at heart1062.co.uk